AN EXPLODED VIEW

also by Michael Longley

NO CONTINUING CITY
(Poems 1963–68)

as editor

CAUSEWAY
(The Arts in Ulster)

UNDER THE MOON: OVER THE STARS
(Children's Verse)

AN EXPLODED VIEW

POEMS 1968–72

by

MICHAEL LONGLEY

LONDON . VICTOR GOLLANCZ LTD . 1973

ISBN 0 575 01666 3

ACKNOWLEDGEMENTS

Some of these poems have appeared previously in *Acorn*; *Antaeus*; *Ariel*; *Atlantis*; *Broadsheet*; *Caret*; *Encounter*; *Hibernia*; *Honest Ulsterman*; *Irish Times*; *Irish Press*; *Listener*; *New Poems 1970–71, 1971–72* (P.E.N.); *New Statesman*; *Phoenix*; *Sphere Book of Modern Irish Poetry*; *Soundings*; *Times Literary Supplement*; *This Week*; and on B.B.C. (Northern Ireland); *Causeway* (B.B.C. Radio 3); *Late Night Line-up* (B.B.C. Television) and Radio Eireann.

Acknowledgements are also due to The Bodley Head and Faber and Faber for permission to print as epigraphs lines from *Stephano Remembers* by James Simmons and *Vergissmeinicht* by Keith Douglas.

Six of the poems, with illustrations by Brian Ferran, were printed in a pamphlet called *Lares* (Poet & Printer, 1972).

PRINTED IN GREAT BRITAIN
BY EBENEZER BAYLIS AND SON LIMITED
THE TRINITY PRESS, WORCESTER, AND LONDON

We are trying to make ourselves heard
Like the lover who mouths obscenities
In his passion, like the condemned man
Who makes a last-minute confession,
Like the child who cries out in the dark.

CONTENTS

AN EXPLODED VIEW

TO THE POETS

The dying fall, the death spasm,
Last words and catechism—

These are the ways we spend our breath,
The epitaphs we lie beneath—

Silent departures going with
The nose flute and the penis sheath.

A NATIVITY

Dog

He will be welcome to
His place in the manger—

Anaesthetist and surgeon
Muffling the child's cries

And biting through the cord
That joins God to Mary.

She-goat

A protective midwife—
She roots out with her horns

A sour cake from the straw
And, jaws grinding sideways,

Devours the afterbirth
Of the child of heaven.

Bullocks

They will make a present
Of their empty purses—

Their perfected music
An interval between

The man with the scissors
And the man with the knife.

12

Bullfinch

Slipped in by an old master
At the edge of the picture—

An idea in Mary's head,
A splash of colour—

Thistle-tweaker, theologian,
Eater-of-thorns.

MISCARRIAGE

A stunned cabin boy
Steering your ship to the bottom,

A flayed finger
Attached almost to the palm of her hand,

A tea leaf
Washed from the rim of her cup,

Unembraceable, indisposable,
My son or my daughter.

LOVE POEM

1

You define with your perfume
Infinitely shifting zones
And print in falls of talcum
The shadow of your foot.

2

Gossamers spun from your teeth,
So many light constructions
Describing as with wet wings
The gully under my tongue.

3

These wide migrations begin
In our seamier districts—
A slumdweller's pigeons
Released from creaking baskets.

LARES
for Raymond Warren

Farls

Cut with a cross, they are propped
Before the fire: it will take

Mug after mug of stewed tea,
Inches of butter to ease

Christ's sojourn in a broken
Oatmeal farl down your throat.

Bridget

Her rush cross over the door
Brings Bridget the cowherd home,

Milk to the dandelion,
Bread to the doorstep, the sun's

Reflection under her foot
Like a stone skimmed on water.

Furrows

My arm supporting your spine
I lay you out beneath me

Until it is your knuckles,
The small bones of foot and hand

Strewing a field where the plough
Swerves and my horses stumble.

Beds

The livestock in the yard first,
Then the cattle in the field

But especially the bees
Shall watch our eyelids lower,

Petal and sod folding back
To make our beds lazy-beds.

Neighbours

Your hand in mine as you sleep
Makes my hand a bad neighbour

Who is moving through stable
And byre, or beside the well

Stooping to skim from your milk
The cream, the dew from your fields.

Patrick

As though it were Christ's ankle
He stoops to soothe in his hand

The stone's underside: whose spine's
That ridge of first potatoes,

Whose face the duckweed spreading
On a perfect reflection.

A rickety chimney suggests
The diminutive stove,
Children perhaps, the pots
And pans adding up to love—

So much concentrated under
The low roof, the windows
Shuttered against snow and wind,
That you would be magnified

(If you were there) by the dark,
Wearing it like an apron
And revolving in your hands
As weather in a glass dome,

The blizzard, the day beyond
And—tiny, barely in focus—
Me disappearing out of view
On probably the only horse,

Cantering off to the right
To collect the week's groceries,
Or to be gone for good
Having drawn across my eyes

Like a curtain all that light
And the snow, my history
Stiffening with the tea towels
Hung outside the door to dry.

THE ROPE-MAKERS

Sometimes you and I are like rope-makers
Twisting straw into a golden cable,
So gradual my walking backwards
You fail to notice when I reach the door,
Each step infinitesimal, a delay,
Neither a coming nor a going when
Across the lane-way I face you still
Or, at large at last in the sunny fields,
Struggle to pick you out of the darkness
Where, close to the dresser, the scrubbed table,
Fingers securing the other end, you
Watch me diminish in a square of light.

DARK GLASSES

Sunlight splintered through the grass,
My own reduced expression,
Your dark glasses
Reflecting these, the whole scene:

Then sounds from the hedgerow, movement
And, behind the flutter of a leaf,
Such designations as
Lighthearted starling, nervous wren.

THE ADULTERER

I have laid my adulteries
Beneath the floorboards, then resettled
The linoleum so that
The pattern aligns exactly,

Or, when I bundled into the cupboard
Their loose limbs, their heads,
I papered over the door
And cut a hole for the handle.

There they sleep with their names,
My other women, their underwear
Disarranged a little,
Their wounds closing slowly.

I have watched in the same cracked cup
Each separate face dissolve,
Their dispositions
Cluster like tea leaves,

Folding a silence about my hands
Which infects the mangle,
The hearth rug, the kitchen chair
I've been meaning to get mended.

Even now I wish that you had been there
Sitting beside me on the riverbank:
The cob and his pen sailing in rhythm
Until their small heads met and the final
Heraldic moment dissolved in ripples.

This was a marriage and a baptism,
A holding of breath, nearly a drowning,
Wings spread wide for balance where he trod,
Her feathers full of water and her neck
Under the water like a bar of light.

GALAPAGOS

Now you have scattered into islands—
Breasts, belly, knees, the mount of Venus,
Each a Galapagos of the mind
Where you, the perfect stranger, prompter
Of throw-backs, of hold-ups in time,

Embody peculiar animals—
The giant tortoise hesitating,
The shy lemur, the iguana's
Slow gaze in which the *Beagle* anchors
With its homesick scientist on board.

BADGER
for Raymond Piper

1

Pushing the wedge of his body
Between cromlech and stone circle,
He excavates down mine shafts
And back into the depths of the hill.

His path straight and narrow
And not like the fox's zig-zags,
The arc of the hare who leaves
A silhouette on the sky line.

Night's silence around his shoulders,
His face lit by the moon, he
Manages the earth with his paws,
Returns underground to die.

2

An intestine taking in
patches of dog's-mercury,
brambles, the bluebell wood;
a heel revolving acorns;
a head with a price on it
brushing cuckoo-spit, goose-grass;
a name that parishes borrow.

For the digger, the earth-dog
It is a difficult delivery
Once the tongs take hold,

Vulnerable his pig's snout
That lifted cow-pats for beetles,
Hedgehogs for the soft meat,

His limbs dragging after them
So many stones turned over,
The trees they tilted.

THE CORNER OF THE EYE

kingfisher

a knife-thrower
hurling himself, a rainbow
fractured against
the plate glass of winter:

his eye a water bead,
lens and meniscus where
the dragonfly drowns,
the water-boatman crawls.

wren

two wings criss-crossing
through gaps and loop-holes,
a mote melting towards
the corner of the eye:

or poised in the thicket
between adulteries,
small spaces circumscribed
by the tilt of his tail.

dipper

the cataract's deluge
and nightmare a curtain
he can go bchind,
heavy water rolling

over feather and eye
its adhesive drops,
beneath his feet the spray
thickening into moss.

robin

breast a warning, he
shadows the heavy-
footed earth-breakers,
bull's hoof, pheasant's toe:

is an eye that would—
if we let it in—scan
the walls for cockroaches,
for bed-bugs the beds.

CASUALTY

Its decline was gradual,
A sequence of explorations
By other animals, each
Looking for the easiest way in—

A surgical removal of the eyes,
A probing of the orifices,
Bitings down through the skin,
Through tracts where the grasses melt,

And the bad air released
In a ceremonious wounding
So slow that more and more
I wanted to get closer to it.

A candid grin, the bones
Accumulating to a diagram
Except for the polished horns,
The immaculate hooves.

And this no final reduction
For the ribs began to scatter,
The wool to move outward
As though hunger still worked there,

As though something that had followed
Fox and crow was desperate for
A last morsel and was
Other than the wind or rain.

READINGS
for Peter Longley

1

I remember your eyes in bandages
And me reading to you like a mother;
Our grubby redeemer, the chimney-sweep
Whose baptism among the sea-weed
Began when he stopped astounded beside
The expensive bed, the white coverlet,
The most beautiful girl he had ever seen—
Her hair on the eiderdown like algae,
Her face a reflection in clean water;
The Irishwoman haunting Tom's shoulder—
The shawl's canopy, the red petticoats
Arriving beside him again and again,
The white feet accompanying his feet,
All of the leafy roads down to the sea.

2

Other faces at the frosty window,
Kay and Gerda in their separate attics;
The icicle driven into Kay's heart—
Then a glance at the pillow where you
Twisted your head again and tried to squeeze
Light like a tear through the bandages.

LETTERS

> *returning over the nightmare ground*
> *we found the place again. . . .*
>
> —KEITH DOUGLAS

1. *To Three Irish Poets*

1

This, the twentieth day of March
In the first year of my middle age,
Sees me the father of a son:
Now let him in your minds sleep on
Lopsided, underprivileged
And, out of his tight burrow edged,

Your godchild while you think of him
Or, if you can't accept the term,
Don't count the damage but instead
Wet, on me, the baby's head:
About his ears our province reels
Pulsating like his fontanel,

And I, with you, when I baptise
Must calculate, must improvise
The holy water and the font,
Anything else that he may want,
And, 'priest of the muses', mock the
Malevolent *deus loci*.

30

Now that the distant islands rise
Out of the corners of my eyes
And the imagination fills
Bog-meadow and surrounding hills,
I find myself addressing you
As though I'd always wanted to:

In order to take you all in
I've had to get beneath your skins,
To colonise you like a land,
To study each distinctive hand
And, by squatter's rights, inhabit
The letters of its alphabet,

Although when I call him Daniel
(Mother and baby doing well),
Lost relations take their places,
Namesakes and receding faces:
Late travellers on the Underground
People my head like a ghost town.

3

Over the cobbles I recall
Cattle clattering to the North Wall
Till morning and the morning's rain
Rinsed out the zig-zags of the brain,
Conducting excrement and fear
Along that lethal thoroughfare:

Now every lost bedraggled field
Like a mythopoeic bog unfolds

Its gelignite and dumdums:
And should the whole idea become
A vegetable run to seed in
Even our suburban garden,

We understudy for the hare's
Disappearance around corners,
The approximate untold barks
Of the otters we call water-dogs—
A dim reflection of ourselves,
A muddy forepaw that dissolves.

4

Blood on the kerbstones, and my mind
Dividing like a pavement,
Cracked by the weeds, by the green grass
That covers our necropolis,
The pity, terror. . . . What comes next
Is a lacuna in the text,

Only blots of ink conceding
Death or blackout as a reading:
For this, his birthday, must confound
Baedekers of the nightmare ground—
And room for him beneath the hedge
With succour, school and heritage

Is made tonight when I append
Each of your names and name a friend:
For yours, then, and the child's sake
I who have heard the waters break
Claim this my country, though today
Timor mortis conturbat me.

2. To James Simmons

We were distracted by too many things . . .
the wine, the jokes, the music, fancy gowns.
We were no good as murderers, we were clowns.

—Who stated with the Irish queer
A preference for girls to beer—
Here's an attempt at telling all,
My confession unilateral:
Not that it matters for my part
Because I have your lines by heart,

Because the poetry you write
Is the flicker of a night-light
Picking out where it is able
Objects on the dressing table,
Glancing through the great indoors
Where love and death debate the chores,

And where, beneath a breast, you see
The blue veins in filigree,
The dust in a glass of water,
In a discarded french letter
The millions acting out their last
Collaborations with the past.

Yes, to entertain your buddies
With such transcendental studies
Rather than harmonise with hams
In yards of penitential psalms
I count among your better turns:
Play your guitar while Derry burns,

Pipe us aboard the sinking ship
Two by two. . . . But before the trip
A pause, please, while the hundredth line
Squanders itself in facile rhyme—
A spry exposé of our game
But paradigmatic all the same

Like talking on as the twelfth chime
Ends nineteen hundred and ninety-nine,
The millennium and number:
For never milestones, but the camber
Dictates this journey till we tire
(So much for perning in a gyre!):

True to no 'kindred points', astride
No iridescent arc besides,
Each gives the other's lines a twist
Over supper, dinner, breakfast
To make a sort of Moebius Band,
Eternal but quotidian. . . .

So, post me some octosyllabics
As redolent of death and sex
Or keep this for the rainy days
When, mindful of the final phase,
We diagnose it a relapse,
A metric following the steps

Of an ageing ballroom dancer
(Words a bow-tie round a cancer):
Or a reasonable way to move—
A Moonlight Saunter out to prove
That poetry, a tongue at play
With lip and tooth, is here to stay,

To exercise in metaphor
Our knockings at the basement door,
A ramrod mounted to invade
The vulva, Hades' palisade,
The Gates of Horn and Ivory
Or the Walls of Londonderry.

3. To Derek Mahon

And did we come into our own
When, minus muse and lexicon,
We traced in August sixty-nine
Our imaginary Peace Line
Around the burnt-out houses of
The Catholics we'd scarcely loved,
Two Sisyphuses come to budge
The sticks and stones of an old grudge,

Two poetic conservatives
In the city of guns and long knives,
Our ears receiving then and there
The stereophonic nightmare
Of the Shankill and the Falls,
Our matches struck on crumbling walls
To light us as we moved at last
Through the back alleys of Belfast?

Why it mattered to have you here
You who journeyed to Inishere
With me, years back, one Easter when
With MacIntyre and the lone Dane
Our footsteps lifted up the larks,
Echoing off those western rocks
And down that darkening arcade
Hung with the failures of our trade,

Will understand. We were tongue-tied
Companions of the island's dead
In the graveyard among the dunes,
Eavesdroppers on conversations

With a Jesus who spoke Irish—
We were strangers in that parish,
Black tea with bacon and cabbage
For our sacraments and pottage,

Dank blankets making up our Lent
Till, islanders ourselves, we bent
Our knees and cut the watery sod
From the lazy-bed where slept a God
We couldn't count among our friends,
Although we'd taken in our hands
Splinters of driftwood nailed and stuck
On the rim of the Atlantic.

That was Good Friday years ago—
How persistent the undertow
Slapped by currachs ferrying stones,
Moonlight glossing the confusions
Of its each bilingual wave—yes,
We would have lingered there for less. . . .
Six islanders for a ten bob note
Rowed us out to the anchored boat.

4. *To Seamus Heaney*

From Carrigskeewaun in Killadoon
I write, although I'll see you soon,
Hoping this fortnight detonates
Your year in the United States,
Offering you by way of welcome
To the sick counties we call home
The mystical point at which I tire
Of Calor gas and a turf fire.

Till we talk again in Belfast
Pleasanter far to leave the past
Across three acres and two brooks
On holiday in a post box
Which dripping fuchsia bells surround,
Its back to the prevailing wind,
And where sanderlings from Iceland
Court the breakers, take my stand,

Disinfecting with a purer air
That small subconscious cottage where
The Irish poet slams his door
On slow-worm, toad and adder:
Beneath these racing skies it is
A tempting stance indeed—*ipsis
Hibernicis hiberniores*—
Except that we know the old stories,

The midden of cracked hurley sticks
Tied to recall the crucifix,
Of broken bones and lost scruples,
The blackened hearth, the blazing gable's

Telltale cinder where we may
Scorch our shins until that day
We sleepwalk through a No Man's Land
Lipreading to an Orange band.

Continually, therefore, we rehearse
Goodbyes to all our characters
And, since both would have it both ways,
On the oily roll of calmer seas
Launch coffin-ship and life-boat,
Body with soul thus kept afloat,
Mind open like a half-door
To the speckled hill, the plovers' shore.

So let it be the lapwing's cry
That lodges in the throat as I
Raise its alarum from the mud,
Seeking for your sake to conclude
Ulster Poet our Union Title
And prolong this sad recital
By leaving careful footprints round
A wind-encircled burial mound.

Here are two pictures from my father's head—
I have kept them like secrets until now:
First, the Ulster Division at the Somme
Going over the top with 'Fuck the Pope!'
'No Surrender!': a boy about to die,
Screaming 'Give 'em one for the Shankill!'
'Wilder than Gurkhas' were my father's words
Of admiration and bewilderment.
Next comes the London-Scottish padre
Resettling kilts with his swagger-stick,
With a stylish backhand and a prayer.
Over a landscape of dead buttocks
My father followed him for fifty years.
At last, a belated casualty,
He said—lead traces flaring till they hurt—
'I am dying for King and Country, slowly.'
I touched his hand, his thin head I touched.

Now, with military honours of a kind,
With his badges, his medals like rainbows,
His spinning compass, I bury beside him
Three teenage soldiers, bellies full of
Bullets and Irish beer, their flies undone.
A packet of Woodbines I throw in,
A lucifer, the Sacred Heart of Jesus
Paralysed as heavy guns put out
The night-light in a nursery for ever;
Also a bus-conductor's uniform—
He collapsed beside his carpet-slippers
Without a murmur, shot through the head
By a shivering boy who wandered in

Before they could turn the television down
Or tidy away the supper dishes.
To the children, to a bewildered wife,
I think 'Sorry Missus' was what he said.

KINDERTOTENLIEDER

There can be no songs for dead children
Near the crazy circle of explosions,
The splintering tangent of the ricochet,

No songs for the children who have become
My unrestricted tenants, fingerprints
Everywhere, teethmarks on this and that.

THE FAIRGROUND

There, in her stall between the tattooist
And the fortune-teller, all day she sits—
The fat lady who through a megaphone
Proclaims her measurements and poundage.
Contortionists, sword-swallowers, fire-eaters

As well as a man with no arms or legs
Who rolls his own cigarettes, managing
Tobacco-pouch, paper, the box of matches
With his mouth: painstaking the performance.
He wears his woollens like a sausage-skin.

Hidden behind the broken-down equipment
Are big foreheads, bow legs, stubby fingers—
Midgets in clowns' make-up and bowler hats:
And in flowered smocks, continuously dancing,
Cretins: a carousel of tiny skulls.

Then a theatrical change in the weather
So that I am the solitary spectator:
A drenched fairground, the company advancing
And it is my head they hold in their hands.
The eyes open and close like a doll's eyes.

NIGHTMARE

In this dream I am carrying a pig,
Cradling in my arms its deceptive grin,
The comfortable folds of its baby limbs,
The feet coyly disposed like a spaniel's.

I am in charge of its delivery,
Taking it somewhere, and feeling oddly
And indissolubly attached to it—
There is nothing I can do about it,

Not even when it bites into my skull
Quite painlessly, and eats my face away,
Its juices corroding my memory,
The chamber of straight lines and purposes,

Until I am carrying everywhere
Always, on a dwindling zig-zag, the pig.

CONFESSIONS OF AN IRISH
ETHER-DRINKER

1

It freezes the puddles,
Films the tongue, its brief lozenge
Lesions of spittle and bile,
Dispersals of weather—

Icicles, bones in the ditch,
The blue sky splintering,
Water's fontanel
Closed like an eyelid.

2

My dialect becomes
Compactings of sea sounds,
The quietest drifts,
Each snowed-under
Cul-de-sac of the brain—
Glaucoma, pins and needles,
Fur on the tongue:

Or the hidden scythe
Probing farther than pain,
Its light buried in my ear,
The seed potatoes
Filling with blood—
Nuggets of darkness,
Silence's ovaries.

POTEEN

Enough running water
To cool the copper worm,
The veins at the wrist,
Vitriol to scorch the throat—

And the brimming hogshead,
Reduced by one noggin-full
Sprinkled on the ground,
Becomes an affair of

Remembered souterrains,
Sunk workshops, out-backs,
The back of the mind—
The whole bog an outhouse

Where, alongside cudgels,
Guns, the informer's ear
We have buried it—
Blood-money, treasure-trove.

Impasto or washes as a rule:
Tuberous clottings, a muddy
Accumulation, internal rhyme—
Fuchsia's droop towards the ground,
The potato and its flower:

Or a continuing drizzle,
Specialisations of light,
Bog-water stretched over sand
In small waves, elisions—
The dialects of silence:

Or, sometimes, in combination
Outlining the bent spines,
The angular limbs of creatures—
Lost minerals colouring
The initial letter, the stance.

THE ISLAND

The one saddle and bit on the island
We set aside for every second Sunday
When the priest rides slowly up from the pier.
Afterwards his boat creaks into the mist.
Or he arrives here nine times out of ten
With the doctor. They will soon be friends.

Visitors are few. A Belgian for instance
Who has told us all about the oven,
Linguists occasionally, and sociologists.
A lapsed Capuchin monk who came to stay
Was first and last to fish the lake for eels.
His carved crucifixes are still on sale.

One ship continues to rust on the rocks.
We stripped it completely of wash-hand basins,
Toilet fitments, its cargo of linoleum
And have set up house in our own fashion.
We can estimate time by the shadow
Of a doorpost inching across the floor.

In the thatch blackbirds rummaging for worms
And our dead submerged beneath the dunes.
We count ourselves historians of sorts
And chronicle all such comings and goings.
We can walk in a day around the island.
We shall reach the horizon and disappear.

Beneath a gas-mantle that the moths bombard,
Light that powders at a touch, dusty wings,
I listen for news through the atmospherics,
A crackle of sea-wrack, spinning driftwood,
Waves like distant traffic, news from home,

Or watch myself, as through a sandy lens,
Materialising out of the heat-shimmers
And finding my way for ever along
The path to this cottage, its windows,
Walls, sun and moon dials, home from home.

CARRIGSKEEWAUN
for David and Penny Cabot

The Mountain

This is ravens' territory, skulls, bones,
The marrow of these boulders supervised
From the upper air: I stand alone here

And seem to gather children about me,
A collection of picnic things, my voice
Filling the district as I call their names.

The Path

With my first step I dislodge the mallards
Whose necks strain over the bog to where
Kittiwakes scrape the waves: then, the circle

Widening, lapwings, curlews, snipe until
I am left with only one swan to nudge
To the far side of its gradual disdain.

The Strand

I discover, remaindered from yesterday,
Cattle tracks, a sanderling's tiny trail,
The footprints of the children and my own

Linking the dunes to the water's edge,
Reducing to sand the dry shells, the toe-
And fingernail parings of the sea.

The Wall

I join all the men who have squatted here
This lichened side of the dry-stone wall
And notice how smoke from our turf fire

Recalls in the cool air above the lake
Steam from a kettle, a tablecloth and
A table she might have already set.

The Lake

Though it will duplicate at any time
The sheep and cattle that wander there,
For a few minutes every evening

Its surface seems tilted to receive
The sun perfectly, the mare and her foal,
The heron, all such special visitors.

SKARA BRAE
for Denis and Sheila Smyth

A window into the ground,
The bumpy lawn in section,
An exploded view
Through middens, through lives,

The thatch of grass roots,
The gravelly roof compounding
Periwinkles, small bones,
A calendar of meals,

The thread between sepulchre
And home a broken necklace,
Knuckles, dice scattering
At the warren's core,

Pebbles the tide washes
That conceded for so long
Living room, the hard beds,
The table made of stone.

GHOST TOWN

I have located it, my ghost town—
A place of interminable afternoons,
Sad cottages, scythes rusting in the thatch;
Of so many hesitant surrenders to
Enfolding bog, the scuts of bog-cotton.

The few residents include one hermit
Persisting with a goat and two kettles
Among the bracken, a nervous spinster
In charge of the post office, a lighthouse-keeper
Who emerges to collect his groceries.

Since no one has got around to it yet
I shall restore the sign which reads CINEMA,
Rescue from the verge of invisibility
The faded stills of the last silent feature—
I shall become the local eccentric:

Already I have retired there to fill
Several gaps in my education—
The weather's ways, a handful of neglected
Pentatonic melodies and, after a while,
Dialect words for the parts of the body.

Indeed, with so much on my hands, family
And friends are definitely not welcome—
Although by the time I am accepted there
(A reputation and my own half-acre)
I shall have written another letter home.

TUTANKHAMUN

That could be me lying there
Surrounded by furniture,
My interest vested in
The persistence of objects,
An affectionate household;
The surrender of the bolt,
The wheeze of dusty hinges
Almost pleasurable
After the prolonged slumber
At my permanent address;
Cerements and substance
A sensational disclosure—
My various faces
Upside down in the spoons.

THREE POSTHUMOUS PIECES

1

In lieu of my famous last words or
The doctor's hushed diagnosis
Lifting like a draught from the door
My oracular pages, this
Will have fluttered on to the floor—
The first of my posthumous pieces.

2

As a sort of accompaniment
Drafted in different-coloured inks
Through several notebooks, this is meant
To read like a riddle from the Sphinx
And not my will and testament—
No matter what anybody thinks.

3

Two minuses become a plus
When, at the very close of play
And with the minimum of fuss,
I shall permit myself to say:
This is my Opus Posthumous—
An inspiration in its way.

ALTERA CITHERA

A change of tune, then,
On another zither,
A new aesthetic, or
The same old songs
That are out of key,
Unwashed by epic oceans
And dipped by love
In lyric waters only?

Given under our hand
(With a ballpoint pen)
After the Latin of Gaius
Sextus Propertius,
An old friend, the shadow
Of his former self
Who—and this I append
Without his permission—

Loaded the dice before
He put them in his sling
And aimed at history,
Bringing to the ground
Like lovers Caesar,
Soldiers, politicians
And all the dreary
Epics of the muscle-bound.

DOCTOR JAZZ

Hello, Central! Give me Doctor Jazz!

Jelly Roll Morton

To be nearly as great as you
Think you are, play the same tunes
Again and again: small fortunes,
Diamonds for each hollow tooth.

Django Reinhardt

A whole new method compensates
For your damaged fingers: sweat
In the creases of your forehead,
Mother-of-pearl between the frets.

King Oliver

Now all pretenders to the throne
Learn how the patient gums decay,
Music hurts: though they took away
Your bad breath, the crown's your own.

Billie Holiday

You fastened to your bony thigh
Some dollar bills and waited for
The cacophonous janitor
And silence and the cue to die.

ALIBIS

1

My botanical studies took me among
Those whom I now consider my ancestors.
I used to appear to them at odd moments—
With buckets of water in the distance, or
At the campfire, my arms full of snowy sticks.
Beech mast, hedgehogs, cresses were my diet,
My medicaments badger grease and dock leaves.
A hard life. Nevertheless, they named after me
A clover that flourished on those distant slopes.
Later I found myself playing saxophone
On the Souza Band's Grand Tour of the World.
Perhaps because so much was happening
I started, in desperation, to keep a diary.
(I have no idea what came over me.)
After that I sat near a sunny window
Waiting for pupils among the music-stands.
At present I am drafting appendices
To lost masterpieces, some of them my own—
Requiems, entertainments for popes and kings.
From time to time I choose to express myself
In this manner, the basic line. Indeed,
My one remaining ambition is to be
The last poet in Europe to find a rhyme.

2

I wanted this to be a lengthy meditation
With myself as the central character—

Official guide through the tall pavilions
Or even the saviour of damaged birds.
I accepted my responsibilities
And was managing daily after matins
And before lunch my stint of composition.
But gradually, as though I had planned it,
And with only a few more pages to go
Of my *Apologia Pro Vita Mea*,
There dawned on me this idea of myself
Clambering aboard an express train full of
Honeymoon couples and football supporters.
I had folded my life like a cheque book,
Wrapped my pyjamas around two noggins
To keep, for a while at least, my visions warm.
Tattered and footloose in my final phase
I improvised on the map of the world
And hurtled to join, among the police files,
My obstreperous bigfisted brothers.

3

I could always have kept myself to myself
And, falling asleep with the light still on,
Reached the quiet conclusion that this
(And this is where I came in) was no more than
The accommodation of different weathers,
Whirlwind tours around the scattered islands,
Telephone calls from the guilty suburbs,
From the back of the mind, a simple question
Of being in two places at the one time.

OPTIONS
for Michael Allen

> *Ha! here's three on 's are sophisticated.*
> *Thou art the thing itself.*

These were my options: firstly
To have gone on and on—
A garrulous correspondence
Between me, the ideal reader
And—a halo to high-light
My head—that outer circle
Of critical intelligences
Deciphering—though with telling
Lacunae—my life-story,
Holding up to the bright mirrors
Of expensive libraries
My candours in palimpsest,
My collected blotting papers.

Or, at a pinch, I could have
Implied in reduced haiku
A world of suffering, swaddled
In white silence like babies
The rows of words, the mono-
Syllabic titles—my brain sore
And, as I struggled to master
The colon, my poet's tongue
Scorched by nicotine and coffee,
By the voracious acids
Of my *Ars Poetica*,
My clenched fist—towards midnight—
A paperweight on the language.

60

Or a species of skinny stanza
Might have materialised
In laborious versions
After the Finnish, for epigraph
The wry juxtaposing of
Wise-cracks by Groucho or Mae West
And the hushed hexameters
Of the right pastoral poet
From the Silver Age—Bacchylides
For instance—the breathings reversed,
The accents wrong mostly—proof—
If such were needed—of my humour
Among the big dictionaries.

These were my options, I say—
Night-lights, will-o'-the-wisps
Out of bog-holes and dark corners
Pointing towards the asylum
Where, for a quid of tobacco
Or a snatch of melody,
I might have cut off my head
In so many words—to borrow
A diagnosis of John Clare's—
Siphoning through the ears
Letters of the alphabet
And, with the vowels and consonants,
My life of make-believe.

IN MEMORY OF GERARD DILLON

1

You walked, all of a sudden, through
The rickety gate which opens
To a scatter of curlews,
An acre of watery light; your grave
A dip in the dunes where sand mislays
The sound of the sea, earth over you
Like a low Irish sky; the sun
An electric light bulb clouded
By the sandy tides, sunlight lost
And found, a message in a bottle.

2

You are a room full of self-portraits,
A face that follows us everywhere;
An ear to the ground listening for
Dead brothers in layers; an eye
Taking in the beautiful predators—
Cats on the windowsill, birds of prey
And, between the diminutive fields,
A dragonfly, wings full of light
Where the road narrows to the last farm.

3

Christening robes, communion dresses,
The shawls of factory workers,
A blind drawn on the Lower Falls.

AN IMAGE FROM PROPERTIUS

My head is melting,
Its cinder burnt for this:

Ankle-bone, knuckle
In the ship of death,

A load five fingers gather
Pondered by the earth.

NOTES

p. 16: This sequence owes much to my reading of *Irish Folk Ways* by E. Estyn Evans (Routledge & Kegan Paul, London, 1957).

p. 29: The stories referred to are Kingsley's *The Water Babies* and Andersen's *The Snow Queen*.

p. 34: The Moebius Band or Strip is an example of a non-orientable surface. It can be illustrated by taking a strip of paper several times longer than it is wide and sticking the two ends together after twisting one of them by a half turn. It is one-sided in the sense that an ant could crawl along the whole length of the strip without crossing the bounding edge and find himself at the starting point on 'the other side'.

p. 39: The Act of Union between Ireland and England became operative in 1801. Positions of privilege granted to those who acquiesced in this are sometimes called Union Titles.

p. 46: Some details in this poem are taken from *Irish Peasant Society* by K. H. Connell (Oxford University Press, London, 1968).

p. 62: The Irish painter Gerard Dillon was born in the Lower Falls district of Belfast in 1916. He died in 1971.